THE
LORD HIMSELF
IS STEPPING IN

HANK KUNNEMAN

One Voice Ministries
P.O. Box 390460
Omaha, NE 68139
855-777-7907
www.hankandbrenda.org

The Lord Himself Is Stepping In
ISBN 978-0-9970645-2-0

TABLE OF CONTENTS

CHAPTER I

Not a Man nor Angel, but the Lord Himself

———

John 5: 2-8 – "Now there is at Jerusalem by the sheep market a pool, which is called in the Hebrew tongue Bethesda, having five porches. In these lay a great multitude of impotent folk, of blind, halt, withered, waiting for the moving of the water. For an angel went down at a certain season into the pool, and troubled the water: whosoever then first after the troubling of the water stepped in was made whole of whatsoever disease he had. And a certain man was there, which had an infirmity thirty and eight years. When Jesus saw him lie, and knew that he had been now a long time in that case, he saith unto him, Wilt thou be made whole? The impotent man answered him, Sir, I have no man, when the water is troubled [angel], to put me into the pool: but while I am coming, another steppeth down before me. Jesus [THE LORD HIMSELF] saith unto him, Rise, take up thy bed, and walk."

Early one morning I was awakened to what sounded like someone speaking directly into my ear. I sat up on my bed to see if the voice I heard had awoke my wife too. She was still asleep, as well as our two German Shepherd dogs that were in our room. At that point I quickly realized it was the Lord speaking to me. He said, "I the Lord, the Lord God Himself is stepping in on behalf of My people!"

The LORD HIMSELF is stepping in.

I immediately went downstairs and began to search the scriptures as to what I heard. I picked up my Bible not sure where to start and noticed that I had turned to John Chapter 5, so I began to read the verses there. I read verses 2-8, understanding the account of a man who had an infirmity for 38 years had come to hopefully get something from the Lord. Would this be his year to be the first and only one in the water as it was being stirred by an angel? After all, the moving of the water only came at a certain season and only the first person in the water was healed. Would this be his season or would he, once again, not make it to the water in time, and while someone else seemed to get the blessing he would be turned away unchanged and with unanswered prayer? His life and his daily routine would then start over until the next opportunity would arise. Sound familiar? For some this is exactly the scenario you have faced. Maybe you have faced this feeling of once again being passed over, while others are getting blessed and receiving breakthroughs and answers to prayers, but you are still waiting. As I read this scripture account I thought about how this applies to a lot of folks. So many waiting for a divine intervention from God, as those who came to hopefully be the first one in the water when the waters would be stirred by the angel so that they might be healed of their condition.

Not a man nor an angel, but the Lord Himself!
I tried to imagine this man, his condition, and what took place that day. How much longer before we see Your intervention, Your glory in the earth, and immediate breakthroughs for Your people, Lord? These were my thoughts as I read this story, only to be interrupted by the voice of the Holy Spirit that continued to speak to me. He said again, "The LORD GOD HIMSELF is stepping in on behalf of His people. It is I stepping in. Not a man nor an angel, but I Myself am stepping in on behalf of My people!" As the Lord was speaking with me I immediately noticed something that I hadn't seen before when I read this passage in scripture. That's it, Lord! It was NOT a man nor an angel, but the Lord Himself that stepped in for this man at the Pool of Bethesda. Now we know that God does use mankind and angels to carry out His blessings. Yet, when you have Jesus standing in front of you that is all you need! It doesn't get any better than that, as there is no one more qualified to take care of us and our needs than Him!

It was the Lord Himself that stepped in for that man and it's the Lord Himself that is stepping in for you. Notice it was not a man nor an angel that brought this man's much needed and awaited breakthrough. In verse 7 the man said, "I have no man," and then further stated, when the waters are stirred [nor angel] as it was an angel that stirred the water. There was no man nor angel, but the Lord Himself standing there to bring this man out of frustration and into a new future, from hopelessness to hope filled days, and from sickness to total wholeness! This was all because of the Lord Himself stepping in, not waiting on man nor angel but instead letting Jesus step in for immediate intervention that would change everything in an instance.

Lord I need help!

This is the same for you and me as we are no different than this man. God said He is stepping in this season and that settles it. We don't have to wait on man nor angelic visitation or intervention. Jesus is stepping in for us in the midst of our cry for help. Now, part of how He steps in may include the prodding or help from man and a carrying out of the Lord's will through His angels. Nevertheless, God has taken our situations and needs to task and is personally stepping in to help! Maybe this is where you are at today as you are facing a situation where you need help. I am here to tell you that The Lord Himself is stepping in to help and is bringing a divine intervention on your behalf!

Remember Peter when He stepped out of the boat with a step of faith, only to sink because He took his eyes off the Lord for just a moment and focused instead on the waves and the wind? However, Jesus didn't let him fall or drown. The Lord Himself reached out and pulled him out of his sinking situation and immediate need for intervention and pulled him up (Matthew 14:26-32). He helped Peter and He has come to help you. Not a man, not an angel, but the Lord Himself is lifting you up and bringing sudden, immediate answers to your prayers.

It's been a long time in my condition.

The key to the Lord's intervention and what helped Peter is to not get too focused on the present crisis or rehearse how long you have been in your condition. Rehearsing how long you have suffered in pain and how long it has been waiting for an answer can cause us to come up emptyhanded. Think for a minute how many times that this man at the Pool of Bethesda had been in his condition. It was 38 long years. Imagine year after year, day after day, and nothing changed. He would walk away without results, without an intervention until the Lord Himself would step in.

He was faced with a choice that day, to give up and accept the same ole routine or choose to do something different. A choice to receive a divine moment that was staring him in the face. It was none other than the Lord Himself.

In the same way we must not pass up our moment of the Lord reaching out and stepping in concerning us and our situations. Let's look for a moment at what this man needed to do that would cause Jesus to step in on his behalf. The Lord asked him a question that would require action on his part. The Lord asked him, *"Wilt thou be made whole?"* (see John 5:6) He is asking us the same thing, will you believe? Will you be healed, made whole, be victorious, and provided for by Him? Will your prayers be answered? In other words, do you see your situation getting better? Do you see a better future and see yourself having the Lord Himself step in on your behalf? He was giving him a choice, wait for a man, wait for an angel, wait for another time, or seize your moment that is right in front of you. After all, Jesus the Lord Himself was standing in front of him ready, willing, and able. This man, like you and me, just needed to take a moment and position himself for a breakthrough and for his intervention!

It wasn't enough for this man to just think about being made whole but to also do something. He had to get up and do something he had not done before. Take a step of faith, seize the moment with his faith and expectation. This is why Jesus would say to him, *"Rise, take up thy bed, and walk."* (John 5:8) It was to allow the Lord to step in for him and to get this man to step forward with an immediate change of life and direction. The waiting period was over, no more delay! No more thinking that he was passed over and passed by from the Lord who loved Him. He needed to seize his moment and we need to seize our moment too! The Lord showed up that day unexpectedly and was poised to step in for this man. The same is true for you and me. We are in a prophetic season and must remember the words the Lord spoke to me that morning, *"The Lord God Himself is stepping in on behalf of My people, on behalf of you!"* This means the moment of our divine intervention from Him has come and everything is about to change for the better. Why? Because the Lord God Himself has come!

CHAPTER 2

When the Doors are Locked!

———

John 20:24-31 – "But Thomas, one of the twelve, called Didymus, was not with them when Jesus came. The other disciples therefore said unto him, We have seen the Lord. But he said unto them, Except I shall see in his hands the print of the nails, and put my finger into the print of the nails, and thrust my hand into his side, I will not believe. And after eight days again his disciples were within, and Thomas with them: then came Jesus [THE LORD HIMSELF], the doors being shut, and stood in the midst, and said, Peace be unto you. Then saith he to Thomas, Reach hither thy finger, and behold my hands; and reach hither thy hand, and thrust it into my side: and be not faithless, but believing. And Thomas answered and said unto him, My Lord and my God. Jesus saith unto him, Thomas, because thou hast seen me, thou hast believed: blessed are they that have not seen, and yet have believed. And many other signs truly did Jesus in the presence of his disciples, which are not written in this book: But these are written, that ye might believe that Jesus is the Christ, the Son of God; and that believing ye might have life through his name."

The doors were shut and, in addition, locked (as many translations mention) as the disciples spent time trying to convince Thomas that they had seen the Lord and that He indeed was alive. Yet, Thomas needed a sign, just as we often feel we do as well. He needed proof to restore his hope and to bring much needed peace. He wanted some supernatural intervention from Jesus to ease his doubts. It had been eight days since the claim from his fellow companions that they had witnessed the Lord's appearing without him. Their experience was not enough for him personally, unless the Lord Himself would step in for him. Yet, how could this be possible when the doors were locked? This would imply that Thomas and the other disciples were not expecting a supernatural intervention or visitation from the Lord, and their fears led them to lock the door. They must have assumed that if the Lord were to appear it would be through the only natural, most expected way, and on their terms through the front door. This would make the most sense after all, right? This would be the only natural solution and would be in accordance with Thomas' terms and conditions of needing a sign that would involve Jesus coming through the front door. Does this sound familiar? It certainly does! It describes the mindset or approach we often take when it comes to the Lord's supernatural intervention or breakthrough in our lives. It is on our terms and conditions with a lot of premeditated thoughts and actions that determine how the Lord is going to show up. It leads us to think that if we do a certain thing then the Lord will do such and such. What they needed to remember, and what we must never forget, is that He was indeed alive and could intervene supernaturally at any given moment. He is not restricted to our conditions, expectations or terms. He is, however, deeply moved by our faith, expectation, and desire for Him to manifest in our lives.

What does this story mean for you and me? It means that the Lord Himself is stepping in on our behalf, just as He did for Thomas. He is coming to show Himself strong and to restore hope and peace even when we have struggled, doubting to believe. An encouraging thing to note is when it seems that doors are shut He will find another way to step in on our behalf! This is exactly what happened for Thomas and is waiting to happen for you!

He defies the doors!
Think about it for a moment, He will find whatever way necessary to step in! He doesn't need the front door, the window, the roof or any other method that we may try to limit Him to.

He will defy the obstacles, the doors, and whatever things that seem closed that are trying to stop the blessing in our lives. This means that He will find a way to show up on our behalf and open up the way for His blessings to come! Closed doors don't stop Him.

He opens doors that no man nor devil can close and closes doors that no man nor demon can open. He will find a way if we are willing to invite Him and believe that He is stepping in on our behalf. What an amazing God, who will find a way to get His blessings to us.

It should be especially encouraging, as with Thomas, that He will defy the doors, finding ways to show His love and power. This means if we have closed the doors through our wrong choices, fears, or even anxiety and worry, He will come ready, opening a new way, as the Lord Himself to step in on our behalf. What about the doors the enemy closes? God will defy even those doors! We certainly know the devil tries to hinder and close doors, after all he tried to hinder and close the door on the Apostle Paul from ministering to those in Thessalonica. 1 Thessalonians 2:18 says, *"Wherefore we would have come unto you, even I Paul, once and again; but Satan hindered us."* Yet that hindrance from the enemy didn't stop God, nor did it stop Paul with the Lord's intervention. This is because the Lord God Himself steps in and defies the devil's attempts to hinder us and stop us, as it was tried with Paul. So, no matter if we have closed the doors or the enemy has, let's always be reminded that even though the door was shut and locked by the disciples in John 20:24-31, it didn't keep the Lord from stepping in another way!

Lord I need a sign!

Maybe you have experienced closed doors and closed heavens. It may seem that things are locked up tighter than a drum concerning you and your situation. It may seem impossible for any supernatural intervention to immediately come, and it has been days and even years waiting for your breakthrough. I want to encourage you to not give up but remember the Lord said that He, the Lord Himself, is stepping in on your behalf. There is something important to remember in the story of Thomas and that is that he needed a sign, something to convince Him that the Lord was indeed intervening in their lives. Now this should not be the norm, nor should it be the pattern for our lives all the time for it is faith that pleases and moves God. Yet there are those times when we are desperate and need encouragement, affirmation, and a boost. Times that we may feel as though the doors are locked and there have not been any sightings of the Lord on our behalf. That's when we look up to heaven and say, "Lord we need a sign, we need some encouragement, and we need immediate and sudden intervention."

We can harp on Thomas and call him the doubting one because he requested a sign, saying unless I see his nail print hands and put my hands in His side, I won't believe. Yes, he should have known better, as should we, because Jesus told him He would rise again. If the Lord said it, He will do it. Yet, what is intriguing is that the Lord did exactly what Thomas was requesting in a sign when He showed up. He told Thomas to touch His nail print hands and put His hands in His side for proof and for evidence that He was very much alive and intervening.

Again, this is not to be the norm, but at those times we need to seize the opportunity for the Lord Himself to show up in our lives immediately and suddenly. When we have reached a place of despair and cry out to the Lord in faith, expecting Him to defy anything that would stand in the way of the Lord Himself stepping in for us!

In the midst of our trials or our waiting we must continue with expectancy, looking for the signs for the Lord Himself to show up. This is why the Lord promised a sign to those who would wait for the birthing of the Messiah that He indeed, the Lord Himself, would give them a sign. Isaiah 7:14 (NIV) says, *"Therefore the Lord himself will give you a sign: The virgin will conceive and give birth to a son, and will call him*

Immanuel." This means that something new is being birthed on our behalf, just like it was with the birth of our precious Messiah, Yeshua, Jesus. It is the Lord Himself stepping in!

The Lord Himself has come to give you peace.

Now we know when our wonderful Redeemer and promised Messiah, the Lord Himself, showed up as the baby born in the manger the declaration was one of peace on earth and goodwill towards men (Luke 2:14). This was the same declaration of peace that Jesus spoke when He stepped in another way with Thomas and the closed door. We see this with the first thing Jesus said in John 20:26, "Peace be unto you." This peace is not only defined as nothing missing and nothing broken, but shalom! Yes, shalom! It is even more extensive, in its definition, than just peace. Shalom is a key word and image for salvation in the Bible, as this Hebrew word refers most commonly to a person being whole, uninjured, and safe. In the Strong's Concordance it is reference number 7965, and its meaning is completeness, wholeness, health, peace, welfare, safety, soundness, tranquility, prosperity, perfectness, fullness, rest, harmony and the absence of agitation or discord.

This means when Jesus entered that room and pronounced shalom He wasn't just pronouncing peace but so much more by the way of His visitation and the full meaning of this word. So, just how does shalom come in our lives and situations? It comes when He, the Lord Himself, steps in. This is why we can say, as the scripture says, *"Now may the Lord of peace Himself continually grant you peace in every circumstance. The Lord be with you all!"* 2 Thessalonians 3:16 (NASB)

We can see from this verse that the Lord wants to continually grant us this peace in every situation. Every situation means every situation! This happens as we choose to stay on the path of peace, guard our hearts and minds, and pray for shalom each day and then we will reap the benefits of this supernatural force! It is so powerful that it calms every storm against us! We saw this with Jesus when a great storm arose against Him and the disciples in the boat. This storm was so violent that the fishermen thought they, along with Jesus, were going to die. Yet how did the Lord respond? He responded by stepping in and declaring to the storm, *"Peace, be still."* (see Mark 4:35-41). This means no matter the situations we face, or the storms raging all around us, we can live and enjoy the benefits of this wonderful shalom. We must remember that it was the Lord Himself that shut Noah and his family in the ark and kept them from a raging storm and flood that lasted for days. It wasn't Noah that shut himself or his family in the ark, but the Lord Himself that came at that divine moment and nothing, absolutely nothing, could remove them from that supernatural place of His peace concerning them (see Genesis 7:16). It was the Lord that shut the door in this case, but it contained His blessing, His provision, His peace, and His protection from the storm raging all around them.

Yet with these examples of the disciples and Jesus, as well as Noah, it doesn't mean that storms will never come to challenge us in our lives, but what it means is we have the Lord Himself that we can call on to calm the storms and help us reach our destiny and His will for our lives. We must never forget this prophetic season we are in where the Lord has promised to step in at this moment and when we understand this we can reap the benefits of what He brings when He shows up.

One of the last words Jesus spoke to His disciples was, *"Peace I leave with you. My peace I give to you, not as the world gives do I give to you."* (John 14:27 NASB) The world cannot give this peace that Jesus came to bring. This is why He said, "Peace I give to you!" Yet people look for all sorts of remedies and substitutes for this supernatural force that can only come from Him. The Lord came to bring a special peace, not a natural peace but His supernatural shalom that can transform our lives and this earth. This peace is not a feeling or emotion because it is supernatural and can exceed any feeling or emotion we might have.

It is so powerful when the Lord steps in that this supernatural peace surpasses all understanding and guards our hearts and minds through Jesus our Lord (see Philippians 4:7-9). This is because sometimes you may have peace in your heart but your mind is not at peace. Sometimes your mind thinks peacefully but your heart is troubled. What God desires is for us to have both peace in our hearts and in our minds and that comes through His shalom.

So no matter what you are facing, the storms might be raging all around you and you feel like you aren't going to see breakthrough. Call out to the Lord and for His peace. Then watch how the Lord God Himself steps in and unlocks doors of blessings and brings His intervention at the very moment you need it! Remember, He has given you His peace and all you need to do is receive it by inviting Him to step in!

CHAPTER 3

The Lord Himself Fights for You!

———

Deuteronomy 3:22 (NIV) "Do not be afraid of them; the Lord your God himself will fight for you."

The Lord God Himself WILL fight for you! That is worth shouting about and is something we must never forget. God is on our side, therefore we have nothing, absolutely nothing to fear. Maybe you are in a battle right now and it has been a long tough fight. The Lord has promised that He Himself will fight on your behalf. This means breakthrough, answered prayer, and victory concerning your battles are on the way. All because He is fighting for you!

Think about this for a moment. The Lord is called a warrior (see Exodus 15:3). He is also called the Lord of Hosts, or in Hebrew, Yahweh Sabaoth, this name is defined as almighty, sovereign, self-existent God over an army of stars, angels, and even creation itself.

It is mentioned 270 times which makes it the most frequently used compound name of God in scripture!

This means there will never be anyone above Jesus or greater than Him. Making Him an experienced fighter against the enemy and, in addition, the commander of angels too numerous to count that minister for those that are heirs of salvation. He is ever present to help us in our times of need and is stepping in for us in this season.

Remember the words I mentioned in Chapter 1 when He spoke that morning He awakened me? "I the Lord, the Lord God Himself, is stepping in on behalf of My people!" In other words, you better get out of my way devil because the Lord Himself is stepping in to fight for me! This ought to cause you to clap your hands and shout unto God with a voice of triumph! Why? Because there is no one more qualified to fight on your behalf but Him! After all, He is the undisputed heavy weight champion of all existence and has never, ever lost a fight. So, when He says that He Himself is stepping in and will fight for you, He means it.

The Lord will fight for you!

There is no greater peace that should flood our hearts than knowing that the Lord Himself will fight for us. The problem is we often tend to try to help Him out or even get in the way of His intervention, and all this does is delay our victories, or even hinder them. We need to stand firm in our faith and what He promised in His word and let Him fight for us. This is why the scripture tells us regarding Israel, that even applies to us today, that the Lord will fight for us and we don't even have to lift a finger! (see Exodus 14:14, TLB) Now this doesn't mean we don't have a part in the process that leads to our victory. It is to remind us that in the midst of the battles we face, it is imperative to watch what we say, keep our attitudes positive and faith filled, while maintaining a position that trusts Him in the heat of the battle. This will keep us from allowing ourselves to doubt Him or His Word, or to complain about our situations. This also gives the Lord access to fight on our behalf as One who is not afraid of a good fight. He is not just any warrior, but the best of them, victorious in battle that proves His might in crushing the heads of his enemies (see Psalm 68:21).

Look at what the Bible says concerning the fighting, warfare nature of this champion. All of these wonderful verses listed below reveal just how much the Lord is on our side and fights on our behalf. He will never leave you nor forsake you. He fights right alongside you and even goes before you to prepare the way so you may experience victory on every side and breakthrough after breakthrough!

> • Isaiah 42:13 (NIV) – *The LORD will march out like a champion, like a warrior he will stir up his zeal; with a shout he will raise the battle cry and will triumph over his enemies.*

> • Psalm 24:8 – *Who is the King of Glory? The Lord strong and mighty, the Lord mighty in battle.*

> • Deuteronomy 20:4 – *For the Lord your God is he that goeth with you, to fight for you against your enemies, to save you.*

• 2 Chronicles 20:15 – ...*Thus saith the Lord unto you, Be not afraid nor dismayed by reason of this great multitude; for the battle is not yours, but God's.*

• Proverbs 21:31 (TLB) - *Go ahead and prepare for the conflict,[a] but victory comes from God.*

• 2 Corinthians 2:14 – *Now thanks be unto God, which always causeth us to triumph in Christ......*

Deuteronomy 1:30 (NASB) says, *"The Lord your God who goes before you will Himself fight on your behalf, just as He did for you in Egypt before your eyes,..."* What does it mean that the Lord will go before you? It means He establishes a shield of protection around you as He prepares the way, causing crooked places to become straight and moves out any obstacles resisting your breakthrough.

Another way we come to understand how the Lord goes before us is that He is the Lord of the breakthrough (see 2 Samuel 5:20). This means He is the One going before us into our battles and He is breaking through demonic hindrances and barriers affecting our lives. This is why when we pray we need to stand our ground believing that we have received the things we have requested of Him. When we do, He clears the way so that we experience answered prayer. The enemy hates it when we pray this way and always remember that all hell fears Jesus, the King of kings and the Lord of lords (see Revelation 19:16). Why does all hell fear Him? Because He is a fierce fighter for His people and is *always* victorious!

The Lord Himself is fighting against the enemy on your behalf.
So when we talk about the Lord stepping in and fighting for us, we have come to understand that He goes before us. He doesn't just go before us to break the enemy's attacks against us, but we also know that He will go behind us to deal with our past and anything trying to sneak up on us. This makes Him our rearguard and keeps us from becoming vulnerable to the enemy's plots and plans concerning us. It also means if we allow God to step in He will help aide us and guard us from living in the memory of our past so we can live in freedom in our present and future!

We see an example of the Lord being our rearguard and His fighting on our behalf in the story of the Children of Israel exiting Egypt, with Moses leading them. Pharaoh and his army quickly began to pursue them with horses and chariots in massive numbers and this caused the Israelites to react in fear, murmuring and complaining. They began to doubt God and doubt that anything better was awaiting them. This caused them to have their eyes more on the enemy's pursuit and attack than on the Lord's blessing of victory. If we are not careful, we tend to resort to the same kind of behavior and can feel that somehow God has forsaken us leaving us to fight our battles alone. Yet that is, and was, the furthest thing from the truth. The Lord, who was actually in front of them in the pillar of cloud, came behind them coming between the armies of Egypt and Israel (see Exodus 14:19), thus becoming their rearguard.

In this season of the Lord Himself stepping in on our behalf we can certainly see the character and pattern He displays of the One who not only goes before us but behind us, and better yet, even surrounds us. In scripture we find that the Lord will fight against the enemy, dealing with them on all sides, bringing them to defeat. Psalm 34:7 says, *"The angel of the Lord encamps around those who fear him, and he delivers them."* We have further hope when we read Psalm 125:2 (NIV), which says, *"As the mountains surround Jerusalem, so the Lord surrounds his people, both now and forevermore."*

Different ways in which the Lord fights for us.
Now that we have discovered that the Lord will never leave us nor forsake us as He goes before us, behind us, and even surrounds us, let's look even closer at how the Lord will actually carry out the battle and bring us to victory. These specific examples will ignite your faith and further give understanding of the Lord Himself coming to step in.

One of the ways is that He neutralizes the enemy, stopping them in their tracks. We see this in the story of Israel, as they were staring the Red Sea in the face while Pharaoh and the Egyptian army were coming fast behind them (see Exodus 14:24-26). This resulted in the Lord overthrowing this powerful enemy and defeating them so badly that they were all washed up! Literally, the Egyptian army washed up on the shore in defeat as the Lord closed the Red Sea upon them after He had opened it for Israel. If He did it for His people, Israel, then He is doing it for you! He is neutralizing your enemy, washing them up in defeat to where they have no power to harm or injure you by any means (see Luke 10:19). Talk about a spiritual immunity that He provides in Him! This is because He is reaching out, stepping in, and troubling the enemy knocking off their chariot wheels (or their pursuit) like He did fighting against the Egyptian army! (see Exodus 14:24-25) This is why no weapon formed against you will prosper, because the Lord is fighting for you and neutralizing the enemy's plans and attacks concerning you.

Something that is vital to remember when we are facing a sure battle and expecting the Lord to step in and fight for us is that we just need to do what Moses did, he lifted his hands and stretched out his rod of authority. How do we do this? We do this when we stand strong in our faith, nothing wavering, and use the God-given right and authority we have as His children. Those God-given rights are declaring His Word, praying prayers of faith, the Blood of Jesus, the Name of Jesus, and the Power of the Holy Spirit, to name a few. When we do, this will result in the Lord Himself stepping in and bringing breakthrough, as we saw in the parting of the Red Sea, and total victory like He did when He took out the army of Egypt!

Another amazing way the Lord steps in to fight on our behalf is through sending confusion, heavenly ambushments, and even a terror that causes our enemies to turn on themselves. This may sound crazy and even humorous, but it is true. Yes, the Lord God will use confusion to trouble our enemies. This is what we find in Exodus 23:27 (AMPC), *"I will send My terror before you and will throw into confusion all the people to whom you shall come, and I will make all your foes turn from you [in flight]."* We can see from this verse that part of the battle strategy of our great Warrior, Jesus Christ, is to send confusion among the demonic hordes of hell. They begin fighting with each other in confusion and in the midst of that confusion turn and run from you in terror. They are no match for our Lord. Deuteronomy 28:7 (NIV) says, *"The LORD will grant that the enemies who rise up against you will be defeated before you. They will come at you from one direction but flee from you in seven."*

Glory to God that our enemies turn and run in opposite directions! As we mentioned previously, another successful way the Lord defeats the enemy on our behalf is that He will send ambushments! What do I mean by ambushments? Just as it is defined: an act or instance of lying concealed so as to attack by surprise. Think about that for a moment, the Lord Himself sending surprise attacks against the enemy and completely annihilating their demonic strategies and plans against us! This means there's nothing that takes our mighty Lord by surprise. 2 Chronicles 20:22 says, *"And when they began to sing and to praise, the Lord set ambushments against the children of Ammon, Moab, and mount Seir, which were come against Judah; and they were smitten."* Notice it was the Lord sending the ambushments against the enemy on their behalf.

This sure brings a new meaning to the scripture that tells us that if God be for us than who can be against us (see Romans 8:34). He is so much for us that in addition to surprise ambushments He will cause our enemies to fight even against themselves. This is what 1 Samuel 14:20 says, *"And Saul and all the people that were with him assembled themselves, and they came to the battle: and, behold, every man's sword was against his fellow, and there was a very great discomfiture."* Can you imagine going out to battle only to see your enemy fighting against one another with their swords? This is exactly what happened as Saul went out to battle, and is one of the great ways the Lord fights on our behalf.

Lastly, as the Lord of Hosts, or the Lord of angel armies, and as a warrior He will often use angelic intervention to gain victory and breakthroughs for His people. Whichever way He chooses I am grateful, as I know you are, that He the Lord Himself is stepping in right now to fight for us! He is shutting the mouths of our enemies, or those things that would try to prey upon us, like He did when He shut the mouths of the Lions concerning Daniel when he was thrown in the lion's den (see Daniel 6).

This is because the Lord is stepping in and fighting for you, and you will see the victory just as He told Jehoshaphat and Israel. We find this in 2 Chronicles 20:17, *"Ye shall not need to fight in this battle: set yourselves, stand ye still, and see the salvation of the Lord with you, O Judah and Jerusalem: fear not, nor be dismayed; to morrow go out against them: for the Lord will be with you."*

What does this mean in the heat of your battles or your current situation? The Lord is stepping in to fight, to bring you into sudden victory. No, not delayed days of continued frustration or despair, but rather immediate results of heaven's transfers concerning you! So be encouraged, the Lord God Himself is stepping in for you! He is fighting for you to bring you into victory and breakthrough after breakthrough!

CHAPTER 4

The Lord Himself Goes Before You!

———

Deuteronomy 31:8 (NIV) – "The Lord himself goes before you and will be with you; he will never leave you nor forsake you. Do not be afraid; do not be discouraged."

Maybe you are in a situation where you feel like throwing in the towel and quitting. You have been in a season of waiting and of continual delay. Perhaps you have found yourself discouraged because of the *"way."* You know, the way things are in your life at this moment and the way things have been going? When the "way" doesn't seem to get any better, it is easy to become quickly discouraged.

This is much like what happened to the children of Israel. They got discouraged because of the "way," or you could say the process. Notice Numbers 21:4 as it describes what was happening with the children of Israel, *"And they journeyed from mount Hor by the way of the Red*

sea, to compass the land of Edom: and the soul of the people was much
discouraged because of the way."

They were not just a little discouraged, as this verse says, they were
much discouraged. Perhaps this describes where you are at, not
just a little discouraged but your soul, meaning your mind, will, and
emotions are much discouraged, just like them. Does your daily and
yearly journey of life seem to not be getting any better?

The Children of Israel were much discouraged in their souls because of
the way of the repetitive cycle day after day, year after year. We know
that what should have taken them only a few days journey out of
Egypt into their promised land took 40 years of a continued cycle of
wandering. The way, speaking of their journey and condition, became
hard, long, and with no apparent end in sight.

Yet, it wasn't because God was somehow being cruel or unavailable
to help them. Much of their discouragement came from their own
actions. How? Well, we know that instead of remembering what the
Lord had promised concerning not leaving them or forsaking them,
they resorted to rehearsing their past days of bondage in Egypt rather
than the new opportunities and blessings the Lord was opening for
them in their promised land. They complained, murmured, and got
angry at God, their process, and the journey of life; causing them, as
we mentioned, to become much discouraged because of the way.

It's time to go northward.
When this level of disappointment, frustration, and discouragement

sets in (like it did with Israel), that is the time to keep our words right and keep pressing for our promised blessings. It is far too easy to speak our minds and say whatever comes to it, letting the promised blessings be hindered yet again. This is what happened to Israel when they had an opportunity to seize their promise for a better day. Instead, they spoke wrong and didn't see the size of the fruit or blessing that God had prepared for them in their promised land. Their discouragement caused them to only see the size of the giant challenges before them. This resulted in reducing themselves, in their own minds, to small thinking. They said they were but grasshoppers compared to the mighty giants in their promised land of blessings (see Numbers 13:30-33). This further led them to forget that the Lord God Himself promised He would not leave them nor forsake them. In addition, He told them that He would fight for them and they were not to be discouraged (see Deuteronomy 31:8).

If they were going to seize their blessings and come out of this cycle of discouragement and wandering, it would require them to change. They would not just need to change their attitude but also their direction. This would require them to start thinking positively, reminding themselves that God was with them. This is why God said in Deuteronomy 2:3, *"You have gone around this mountain long enough now turn and go northward."*

The Lord was telling them that they were going around the same ole mountain long enough, now it was time for them to change and go northward. Why northward? It was to get them back on course to their promised land. However, for you and me, north prophetically speaking is the direction and place of heaven. The Lord was drawing attention to the fact that they were wandering in a path contrary to Him and contrary to His blessings because they were allowing discouragement to dictate their journey. By them adjusting their attitude and their direction to go northward it would align them for His blessing and bring them out of this cycle of discouraged wandering. In the same way the more we allow our mind, will, and emotions to dictate our attitudes and our focus (or path) we will get off course just like them. Instead, we need to look to God, look to heaven's blessings and know that the Lord Himself is stepping in to bring us into a new season and a better day. This is what He has promised and why He is speaking right now at this moment to us that He Himself is stepping in!

It's never too late to adjust our lives and go northward toward the way of heaven's blessings, and a life filled with the promises of His Word. This starts by deciding to put discouragement and frustration to the side and becoming spiritually minded, seeing God at work in our situations. In order to do this, we need to position ourselves with great expectation that He is actually stepping in to bring us into our promised season. This will result in sudden, immediate answers to prayer and breakthrough that breaks every hindrance against us or any delay!

So, are you ready to start turning northward toward a new way of thinking, speaking, and walking with heaven's blessing? If so, then decide that the direction of wandering, frustration, and living in discouragement has reached a place in your life where you've had enough. It's time to change the negative words of complaining, any negative mindset about ourselves or situation that brings discouragement, and decide to go northward.

Encourage yourself in the Lord your God.

This is exactly what King David had to do. He had to decide to go northward and not allow himself to become much discouraged. This is because he and his mighty men, after a time of battle, were finally coming back to their families in Ziklag. Except there was something wrong, something didn't seem right and the sky was filled with black smoke and the smell of fire filled the air as they approached closer to their homes. Their homes had been burned and their wives, children, and animals had been taken by their enemy. David's mighty men could hardly believe what they were seeing and experiencing. The pain of their loss, their suffering, and the fear of what had happened to their family gripped their souls, so much to the point they all began to weep bitterly until they could cry no more. Their souls were so deeply discouraged that they even considered killing their leader, David, by stoning (see 2 Samuel). Yet, David did something that is the key for you and me. He sought the Lord expecting the Lord God Himself to step in on their behalf. What was his secret? What did David do to position himself out of the pit of discouragement and despair? He turned northward to God and did the opposite of discouragement. He encouraged himself in the name of the Lord "his" God as we find in 1 Samuel 30:6.

He did the opposite of discouragement, he encouraged himself. Notice it wasn't just that he encouraged himself but encouraged himself in the Lord "his" God. What is the difference? He had a revelation of the Lord for himself, not based on what others told him or maybe what he had heard or read. He had real experiences with God that he drew to his remembrance and rehearsed those victories of when God pulled him through, like with the lion and the bear for example (see 1 Samuel 17). This is why Jesus asked the disciples, who do men say that I am? They could tell Him what others said about who He was, but they lacked revelation for themselves. Jesus wasn't satisfied with their answer and followed up by asking, who do you say that I am? In other words, who am I to you personally? Peter was the only one, like David, that had a revelation of God for himself at a deeper level. He said, Lord you are the Son of the living God (see Matthew 16:16.) In the same way, when we are discouraged that's the time to rehearse who God is for us personally and how He has been loving, healing, caring, and providing for us time and time again. If David could do this in the midst of his pain and trial of having his family kidnapped, possessions taken, and home burned with fire then you and I can certainly draw on the Lord and His encouragement for us as well.

So, just what causes discouragement to come into our lives? Discouragement sets in when things don't seem to be going right in our life's journeys. The result is that we start to get negative and see the glass half empty instead of half full. We often talk wrong by complaining, which causes us to regress, and even for some to stop reading their Bibles, praying, attending church, and even stop serving God altogether. When discouraged, it is often human nature to regress and stop building, dreaming, pushing, or even trying. Sometimes when discouragement hits, people can began to quit caring about things they enjoy and cherish, including themselves. This can result in over compulsion of eating, not caring how they look or dress and they hit a downward spiral into a life that feels too low to be able to get up any higher! When a place of despair or discouragement like that hits it is definitely time to do what David did and that is to encourage yourself in who God is and has been to you.

This is important because discouragement can come to render us ineffective in our lives. As mentioned, it can cause us to feel like quitting, as we saw with Israel when they became discouraged because of the way (see Numbers 21:4.) The word discouraged in this verse is to imply quitting. In addition, discouragement can also seek to neutralize us in our purpose and attitude, resulting in staying in the place of mediocrity and never reaching our promise. This is exactly another type of discouragement that affected some of those in Israel who became neutralized in their pursuit. It's why Moses said unto some of the children of Israel, why do you sit here while your brethren go to war and why do you discourage others from crossing over into their inheritance? (see Numbers 32:6-7) We can see from this verse that the definition of discouragement is to neutralize and that is exactly what happened to some of them. If that wasn't bad enough, they were now negatively affecting others with the same kind of discouragement as themselves. We can certainly see the dangerous affects it causes as it keeps us from having a breakthrough and from pressing forward.

In order to not fall prey to these kinds of discouragements we must be reminded that the Lord doesn't want us to wander in a never ending pattern of frustration, despair, and discouragement like they did. In fact, Jesus's message to us today is always that which He spoke in Matthew 14:27, "*Be of good cheer; it is I; be not afraid.*" And also what He spoke in John 16:33, "*These things I have spoken unto you, that in me ye might have peace. In the world ye shall have tribulation: but be of good cheer; I have overcome the world.*" In other words, no matter what, don't lose hope but stay encouraged because the Lord God Himself is stepping in!

We must continue to declare, from our lips, that God is for us and He Himself is intervening on our behalf. When we do this, we silence the negative voices that try to discourage us. This is why encouraging ourselves in the Lord requires the silencing of the voice of discouragement and not allowing it to grip our lives. We must be aware and wise concerning discouragement. It can be dangerous! It has a voice! Yet, we need to be determined more than ever to say from our mouths, "I am not quitting, I am strong in the Lord, I am full of His peace concerning me, and best of all the Lord God Himself is stepping in right now for me! I will not be discouraged because the Lord will not leave me nor forsake me. The Lord God Himself is stepping in for me!"

CHAPTER 5

The Lord Himself Will Provide!

———

Genesis 22:7-8 (NIV) – Isaac spoke up and said to his father Abraham,
"Father?" "Yes, my son?" Abraham replied. "The fire and wood are here,"
Isaac said, "but where is the lamb for the burnt offering?" Abraham
answered, "God himself will provide the lamb for the burnt offering, my
son." And the two of them went on together.

God Himself will provide! That is exactly what the Lord is saying and emphasizing concerning you and His people. The season of delay, lack, and struggle are coming to an end. There is a better day for you and it is in this now season. This is exactly what the prophet Elisha spoke when he prophesied by saying, "This time tomorrow!" In other words, the season of lack, famine, and struggle were coming to anend! (See 2 Kings 7:1) This was because the Lord had announced and declared through His messenger that He was stepping in to cause an immediate change to a long harsh season of famine. In the same way, God is speaking this to His people right now. He is once again declaring, "This time tomorrow things are going to change." Why? Because the Lord God Himself is stepping in!

This is why it is not the hour to rehearse the bad or what isn't happening in your life, but rather to come into agreement with what the Lord is speaking prophetically. He has declared that He, the Lord God Himself, is stepping in at this time. So this means we need to be expecting that this time tomorrow things are going to change for the better just like Elisha prophesied.

You might be saying, "I sure hope things will get better because I have been in a great season of lack and famine where it seems there is no end in sight." You might feel as though you have sacrificed everything and have given until it hurts and you are still struggling to have your needs met. Sure, this may be the way things are going right now or have been, however when you are in a prophetic season of the Lord's choosing everything changes. So much in fact that these changes are drastic, immediate, and suddenly! We must not forget that we can never out give God and He does notice when we truly give our best to Him, especially in a time of lack or hardship. This is exactly what Abraham did as he offered his best to the Lord. He did this by taking Isaac his son and offering him for a sacrifice as the Lord instructed. This got God's attention as he gave his very best in his son, and the Lord saw his willingness to give him for a sacrifice if needed. However, God already had a plan in place for a sudden, immediate provision. This is why when Abraham said, "Surely the Lord God Himself will provide," it was immediately thereafter that the Lord did provide for the sacrifice, by causing the provision to manifest in a ram that became caught in the thicket. This ram would be the Lord's provision that was the sacrifice needed instead of his son Isaac (see Genesis Chapter 22). We can learn from this example that we must be willing to give our best and our all to the Lord, then He will always reward our sacrifice that we give to Him by providing for us, even if it seems like it is last minute.

The Lord Himself will provide.

What is important in this story with Abraham is that he had a confidence in the Lord and His provision that we need to keep in mind. God is not a respecter of persons, meaning that if He provided for him then He will provide for you! This is why we need to say, as Abraham said, "The Lord Himself will provide." We need to say that every day, "The Lord God Himself will provide, The Lord God Himself will provide." When you do, watch how God suddenly breaks forth and brings immediate blessings of provision. If we will incorporate this kind of speaking of provision and also express this kind of heart of giving that Abraham had, then we will be able to say, "My God shall supply all of my need....." (See Philippians 4:19)

This is why it is important that we have the same confidence like Abraham, who believed that the Lord Himself was going to provide. One of the reasons he believed this was because of a revelation that he had of something the Lord said to him prior to this time of offering Isaac as a sacrifice. This happened when God came and visited Abraham, introducing Himself as the Lord who would bless and reward him. The Lord spoke this in Genesis 15:1, *"After these things the word of the Lord came unto Abram in a vision, saying, Fear not, Abram: I am thy shield, and thy exceeding great reward."* The word reward can be translated salary, payment, compensation, benefit, or wage. Perhaps this explains why Abraham's immediate response was, "what will you give me....?" (see Genesis 15:2)

We can see that the Lord was revealing to Abraham that He is a good God and wants to bless and reward us as His children. We must never stop trusting His provision because our Heavenly Father is committed to our needs and to our care. This is what Psalm 100:3 (NASB) says, *"Know that the Lord Himself is God; It is He who has made us, and not we ourselves; we are His people and the sheep of His pasture."* This means that the Lord Himself will take care of us, protecting, feeding, and caring for us as a good shepherd. This shouldn't be a surprise as Jesus referred to Himself as the good shepherd, saying, *"I am the good shepherd"* (see John 10:11). What does this mean for you and me? It means the Lord, as the good shepherd, is helping and stepping in on our behalf. He is showing His goodness to us as He watches over and cares for our every need. This is why we can say with surety, *"The Lord is our shepherd we shall not want for any good thing and He provides for us as he leads us into green pastures."*(Psalm 23)

The Lord Himself is descending on your behalf.
We must trust the Lord's goodness, His tender care and provision as the wonderful good Shepherd! It is vital that we come to understand that the Lord is not just referred to as our good shepherd in scripture but He is also called Jehovah the good! We find this in 2 Chronicles 30:18 – where it says, "But Hezekiah prayed for them, saying, The

THE LORD HIMSELF IS STEPPING IN

good LORD pardon everyone." This Hebrew definition for "good Lord" is translated as Jehovah the good! This means He is a good God! In fact, He is not just good but He is great, and He is an ever present help to us in our time of need!

This is why the days of bareness, famine, and lack are coming to an end. This is because we are in such a prophetic season where we are seeing the goodness of God in such an amazing way, especially in His provision concerning us. As He has declared, He is manifesting Himself in this time to show His goodness! The way He is doing this is by descending on our behalf as the Lord God Himself right here and right now, ever present to help us! We often quote the scripture that declares He is descending in reference to His second coming, as it declares the Lord Himself shall descend from Heaven with a shout and with the voice of the archangel, and with the trumpet of God: and the dead in Christ shall rise first (see 1 Thessalonians 4:16-17). Understanding this passage of scripture speaks of His soon return, yet is it possible that He would descend before this time in a purposeful and unique way, to step in on our behalf for such a time as this? The answer to that is an absolute yes! This is exactly what He is doing. He is descending, as we have discussed, to personally help us, to intervene, open doors, fight for us, encourage us, and provide for us!

This is why we can declare with confidence that the Lord Himself is descending on our behalf right now and is bringing sudden and immediate provisions and answers to prayers! Let's not forget those ever important words that He spoke, the Lord God Himself is stepping in on behalf of His people. We need to speak those words and rehearse them, followed up with a continued life of giving to Him and others. When we do we release the Lord's blessings in an unprecedented way. I want you to think for a moment what happens when the Lord steps in. When He does, He causes nothing to turn into something that brings blessings! We find that those blessings are far too numerous to count when He comes on the scene. This is why the scripture even tells us that He blesses us exceedingly, abundantly beyond all we could ask or think! (See Ephesians 3:20)

We find this example of abundant blessings breaking forth when the Lord steps in. It is found in the story when Jesus came to Peter who had been fishing all night and had caught nothing (see Luke Chapter 5). Yet something shifted immediately and abundantly when Jesus showed up on the scene. When the Lord God Himself showed up nothing became something! How did this happen? It happened after Jesus told him to let down the fishing nets again. When Peter obeyed, the nets broke because of an exceeding abundant catch beyond what they expected. Why did this happen? Was it because Peter was a great fisherman or because the Lord God Himself stepped in? We know the answer! It was because Jesus Himself stepped in on his behalf just like He is for you, as we have been discovering throughout this book. He has spoken prophetically that He is stepping in now. So we need to obey that word and start launching out in the deep, like Peter did with his net, and not make excuses. If we want results like this then we need to do what he and Abraham did. We need to be faithful in our giving to God and to others. Stinginess and a bad attitude about life and giving do not position us for blessings. It is only when we have the right heart followed by action to give our best to the Lord that we position Him to step in on our behalf. How do we get the results of Peter? We do the same thing he did, we take a bold and obedient step and launch forth with our giving, our praise, thanksgiving, and speaking His blessings.

This is why we can see from the example with Peter that Jesus was trying to get him to give his net. This net would become a necessary offering that would produce the Lord God Himself to step in on Peter's behalf. I encourage you to start looking at what you have and not at what you don't have and be willing to give it as a sacrifice of heartfelt offering to the Lord. When we do, we will see our nets break as Peter did and the result will be an abundant blessing in return. This is so vital to remember when we are faced with a need and we are so desperately waiting for the Lord to step in. The answer to our breakthrough is found in our giving. In other words, our giving of our tithes and offerings to God faithfully will unlock the windows of heaven, and just like with the net of Peter we too will see results of such breakthrough of the Lord's provision and blessing. It is because we gave something in our time of need as Peter did with his net. When you give in the time of need, I encourage you to watch as nothing turns to something as the Lord God Himself steps in to provide and bless you in a tremendous way!

And the Lord did so.

It is not uncommon for the Lord to do something so awesome like He did with Peter and with Abraham to provide for them. He is poised to do this for you as well. He wants to bless you and what concerns you, so that you can say from your mouth, the Lord did so for me! This is exactly what happened with the Children of Israel as God favored them so much by putting a separation from them and the people of Israel. It is as Exodus 8:23 says, *"And I will put a division between my people and thy people: to morrow shall this sign be."*

This is such an amazing blessing from the Lord for His people, but also for you in this important season of the Lord God Himself stepping in and favoring His people. We will then be able to confidently say, as the next verse declares in Exodus 8:24, *".......and the Lord did so..."*

Start saying that now concerning your life, your needs, or whatever you might be needing concerning the Lord's provision and intervention. Keep saying, "The Lord did so! The Lord did so concerning me!" When you do you release divine favor and provision for the Lord to come immediately and act on your behalf. It is never too late to start establishing a life of right thinking, right speaking, and faithful giving. Be encouraged that the Lord did so concerning you! Why? Because the Lord Himself is stepping in on your behalf!